What a
Great Idea!

by Sharon Franklin

illustrated by Victor Kennedy

Editorial Offices: Glenview, Illinois • Parsippany, New Jersey • New York, New York
Sales Offices: Needham, Massachusetts • Duluth, Georgia • Glenview, Illinois
Coppell, Texas • Ontario, California • Mesa, Arizona

Every effort has been made to secure permission and provide appropriate credit for photographic material. The publisher deeply regrets any omission and pledges to correct errors called to its attention in subsequent editions.

Unless otherwise acknowledged, all photographs are the property of Scott Foresman, a division of Pearson Education.

Photo locators denoted as follows: Top (T), Center (C), Bottom (B), Left (L), Right (R), Background (Bkgd)

Illustrations by Victor Kennedy

Photographs: 4 Corbis; 5 Corbis; 7 Library of Congress; 12 Getty Images; 13 AP/Wide World Photos

ISBN: 0-328-13532-1

7 8 9 10 V0G1 14 13 12 11 10 09 08

TABLE OF CONTENTS

Chapter One Three Young Inventors

What do you think of when you hear the word *inventor*? Maybe you think of someone working hard in a laboratory. Perhaps you see a person bent over a computer, with tools lying all around. Or possibly, you see an image of Ben Franklin, Thomas Edison, or George Washington Carver.

Would it surprise you to learn that kids are inventors too? Young people have been inventing for a very long time. Keep reading to find out about the great ideas that kids have come up with.

This painting shows Japanese women making silk.

Hsi Ling Shi Invents Silk

Five thousand years ago, a fourteen-year-old Chinese empress named Hsi Ling Shi invented the process of weaving silk. It all started when a silkworm cocoon fell from a tree into a cup of tea that Hsi Ling Shi was drinking.

Hsi Ling Shi saw that threads appeared when the cocoon came apart in the tea. She pulled on the threads. They were very strong! Hsi Ling Shi used the threads to weave fabric. The fabric was strong, soft, and beautiful.

Soon, her Chinese **subjects** began weaving silk. Merchants from faraway countries came to China to buy silk, since only the Chinese knew how to make it. All of this was started by a fourteen-year-old girl!

Silkworms spin cocoons made out of silk.

Chester's Earmuffs

Thousands of years after Hsi Ling Shi invented silk, fifteen-year-old Chester Greenwood invented earmuffs. Chester lived in Maine, a state that has cold winters. Chester's ears got so cold that he could only play outside for brief periods of time.

Chester wanted to keep playing outside without his ears getting cold. Then he got an idea! He bent a piece of wire to the shape of his head. He asked his grandmother to sew two circles padded with fabric. Chester attached the circles to the ends of the wires. Then he put his creation onto his head!

At first, people thought Chester looked funny with his earmuffs. But when they saw how long he could stay out in the cold, they looked at him **admiringly**. Soon, people were buying earmuffs from Chester!

Chester Greenwood didn't stop at earmuffs. He was eventually awarded more than one hundred patents for his inventions.

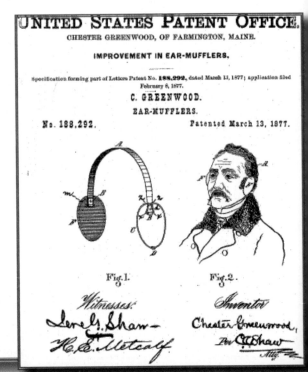

Chester Greenwood is wearing his invention.

Jeanie Low Reaches High

Most people would find it frustrating having to struggle to reach up to a sink. Jeanie Low isn't most people. She invented the Kiddie Stool!

When Jeanie was little, she had to stand on a stool to reach the sink in her house. But Jeanie's parents bumped into the stool when they used the sink, which created a problem.

Jeanie wanted a stool that wouldn't be in the way. She realized that a step that folded up against the sink cabinet might work. She could fold the step down when she needed it. When she didn't need it, she could fold it up flat against the cabinet. Then her parents could use the sink without bumping into anything!

Jeanie Low became famous for her invention.

At first, Jeanie thought she could use wire to attach the step. But she realized that wire could be dangerous. Then Jeanie figured out that magnets would **permit** her to keep the step in place.

Jeanie and her dad gathered some supplies. Together, they built and tested a Kiddie Stool. It worked!

Around the same time, Jeanie's school had a fair where students could display their inventions. Jeanie entered her Kiddie Stool and won first prize!

Soon, Jeanie was appearing on TV to talk about her invention. People wrote articles about her. Jeanie became interested in inventing other things. She joined an inventors' club where she could talk with other people about her ideas.

The Kiddie Stool

Chapter Two The Patent Process

Do you remember that Chester Greenwood got a patent for his earmuffs? That was so no one else could make and sell earmuffs. Chester didn't want any **scoundrels** to copy or make money from his invention. Jeanie also got a patent for her Kiddie Stool.

There are several steps required to get a patent. You have to show that no one else has come up with your invention before you.

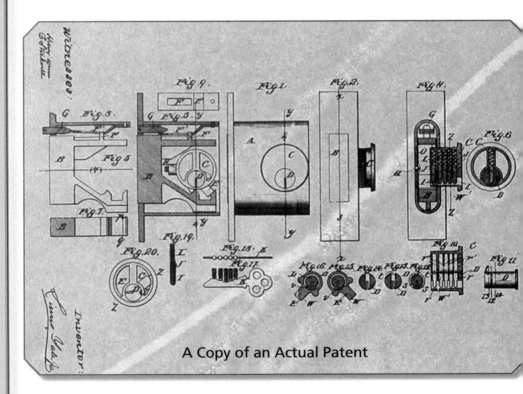

A Copy of an Actual Patent

This patent is for a lock and key.
Patents can protect your ideas.

Getting a patent takes time and money. Serious inventors usually hire lawyers. These lawyers make sure that no one else has had the same idea and applied for a patent. They also help fill out the patent application correctly.

Jeanie and her parents had to go through all the steps in the chart below before Jeannie got her patent. When she was ten years old, Jeanie became one of the youngest patent holders ever!

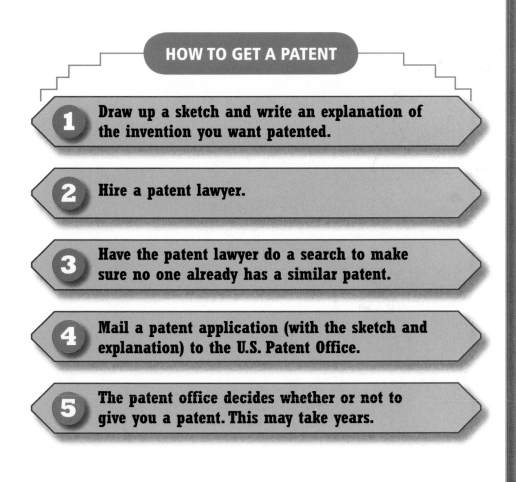

HOW TO GET A PATENT

1 Draw up a sketch and write an explanation of the invention you want patented.

2 Hire a patent lawyer.

3 Have the patent lawyer do a search to make sure no one already has a similar patent.

4 Mail a patent application (with the sketch and explanation) to the U.S. Patent Office.

5 The patent office decides whether or not to give you a patent. This may take years.

Chapter Three More Young Inventors

Inventing to Help a Friend

Josh Parsons was a ten-year-old baseball player when he became an inventor. He wanted to help someone who was having difficulty in sports.

Josh's dad was a baseball coach. He told Josh about a young boy named David who wanted to be on the team. David's arms had been amputated, or removed by surgery, around the elbows. Despite this handicap, David had learned to catch and bat a ball. But he could not throw.

Jim Abbott

Josh thought he could make something that would help David throw. David had found a way to attach a baseball mitt to the end of one of his elbows. He could catch with it. Josh thought that a scoop on the other arm might allow David to throw the ball. He did some experiments with paper to test his idea. Then he sewed a scoop out of leather.

David tried on Josh's invention. First, he caught the ball. Then he put the ball into the scoop on his other arm. Finally, he swung his arm so that the ball went flying out of the scoop. It worked! Thanks to Josh's invention, David made the team.

Pete Gray

Like David, Jim Abbott and Pete Gray were disabled baseball players. Both played in the major leagues.

Inventing for the Fun of It

Jeanie Low's younger sister, Elizabeth, is also an inventor. One day, Elizabeth was visiting her father at his medical office. Elizabeth was only four years old, but she wanted to enter an invention in that year's invention fair. Then she spotted the rubber gloves her father wore to examine patients. They gave her an idea!

Elizabeth took some gloves home and filled them with sand. She bent the fingers. Then she decorated the outsides so they looked fun and cheery.

Elizabeth Low invented
Happy Hands.

Elizabeth named her invention Happy Hands and took it to the invention fair. She told people her Happy Hands could be used as paperweights or to hold toys, jewelry, or other supplies. The judges liked Elizabeth's invention, and they gave her first prize!

So many people were interested in Elizabeth's Happy Hands that she decided to patent her idea. When Elizabeth was nine, she received a patent for Happy Hands. That made her an even younger patent holder than her sister Jeanie!

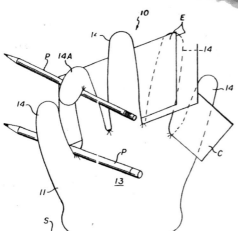

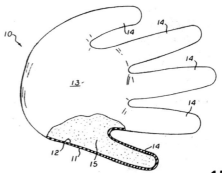

Chapter Four You Too Can Be an Inventor!

Josh Parsons and the Low sisters are just a few of our country's young inventors. Every year, students just like you enter invention fairs. Many of these students go on to other fairs and contests. And a few are awarded patents for their inventions!

Would you like to be an inventor? Inventing can be enjoyable and rewarding. Think of the fun and pleasure you could give people by inventing something that no one has ever thought of!

Would you like to give it a try? The list on page 17 describes the steps you need to take. Read the list carefully. Then read the helpful hints on pages 18 and 19. Can you imagine going through this process?

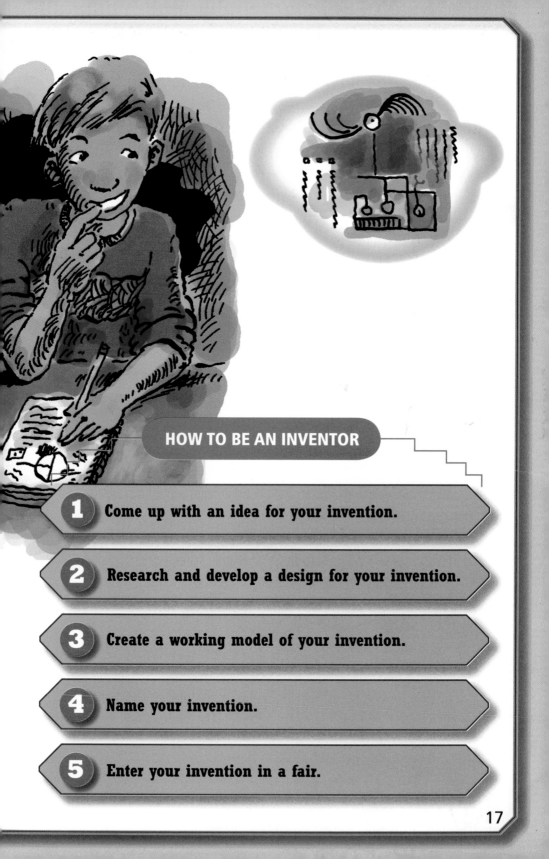

HOW TO BE AN INVENTOR

1 Come up with an idea for your invention.

2 Research and develop a design for your invention.

3 Create a working model of your invention.

4 Name your invention.

5 Enter your invention in a fair.

Putting It All Together

To start the flow of good ideas, you have to be on the lookout for things that could be turned into inventions. Carry a pencil and a notebook with you. When an idea strikes, jot it down right away! A quick sketch will help you remember your thoughts.

Browse through library books to read about inventors and their inventions. Use an Internet search engine to find information on the Web.

Jot down your ideas in a notebook.

Do research to find out if your idea has already been patented. It would be **worthless** for you to do a lot of work, only to find out that someone has already invented and patented your idea! If your idea hasn't been patented, make a detailed sketch. Also, explain how it works. Then you can have your parents or your teacher help you fill out a patent application.

The most important thing is to have confidence in your ideas. Why not give inventing a try? Who knows, you just might become the next Elizabeth Low or Chester Greenwood!

Jeanie Low's
Kiddie Stool

Elizabeth Low's
Happy Hands

Glossary

admiringly *adv.* with wonder, pleasure, and approval.

permit *v.* to let; allow.

scoundrels *n.* evil, dishonorable people; villains; rascals.

subjects *n.* people who are under the power, control, or influence of others, as subjects of a king or queen.

worthless *adj.* without value; good-for-nothing; useless.